SPY 101 ™

TRICKS OF THE TRADE

by Matt Payne

SCHOLASTIC INC.

CONTENTS

CALLING ALL SECRET AGENTS!

DO YOU HAVE WHAT IT TAKES?

HEY, YOU! Yes, you—the kid hiding in a dark alleyway with an oversized trench coat and dark hat.

I can see from your outfit that you're looking to take the first step toward a career in espionage. Well, you've come to the right place!

Read on for the ultimate spy tips and tricks!

Dig into information on surveillance, stakeouts, and tailing techniques that will help you pick up juicy facts about your targets. Learn about covert communication and codes to keep your secrets. Go deep undercover, and explore the latest in high-tech cyber espionage. Go back in time to awesome moments in spy

Find out how to hide your identity— spy style!

history, and get the scoop on some of the coolest spies ever.

By the end of this book, you'll have everything you need for your next spy mission. If you need a little practice before you head out, there are even activities!

NOTES

Learn the secrets behind even the most difficult-to-decipher coded messages!

Uncover the best ways to pass along secret information to fellow spies!

LISTEN...
WITHOUT BEING SEEN!

Audio Surveillance

What happens when spies are dying to eavesdrop on a secret conversation but can't get into the room?

SPY LINGO
SURVEILLANCE: Keeping a close watch on a suspect.

They just "plant a bug"— spy lingo for hiding a small microphone—and listen in!

But how do they get in without being noticed?

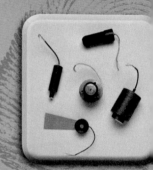

Lock-Picking

Folks with secrets are really good at locking their doors. One of the main tools in a good spy's bag of tricks is a handy lock-picking kit like this one. These kits make it easy to break into many locked rooms.

An unpickable lock? No problem! They try ...

Wiretapping

Spies can secretly listen to a landline telephone conversation (known as "wiretapping") at any point along the path the phone call travels! They simply tap into the cable outside of the house, directly into a utility box, or even into huge banks of telephone switches.

Or, if there's no telephone, and they can wait . . .

This photo shows a re-creation of a radio intercept room used by British intelligence during WWII.

THEY BUILD A BUG INTO A PIECE OF FURNITURE or anything else being delivered to the secret room!

Just find out when the delivery is taking place, and then hide the bug before it gets inside!

A History of Espionage

During the Cold War, the embassy built for America by the Russians was filled with bugs. And you thought bedbugs were bad!

WHY DO I FEEL LIKE SOMEBODY'S WATCHING ME?

Stakeouts and Tails

What's the best way for spies to gather information? By just keeping their eyes open!

STAKEOUT!

Secretly watching a target from a nearby house, office, or parked car is known as a "stakeout."

Most of the time during a stakeout will be spent waiting for the target to do something interesting.

TRICKS OF THE TRADE

Tip One: Location! Location! Location! Choose a spot that has a direct line of sight to the target's activities. The ideal spot can be entered and exited from the back, to minimize the chances that the target will see you arriving or leaving.

Tip Two: Get equipped! You'll need a good field telescope, binoculars, or some other viewing device. If it's an overnight stakeout, you'll need night-vision binoculars. Don't forget your digital camera so you can record anything suspicious.

Tip Three: Good spies know to bring a snack . . . and lots of patience!

TAILING A TARGET

GPS Tracker

Spies can track targets from the comfort of their own home, thanks to the marvels of modern technology.

TRICKS OF THE TRADE

Tip One: Never take your eyes off a target.

Tip Two: Walk on the opposite side of the street.

Tip Three: If the target turns around and looks at you, just act natural. Don't panic!

Tip Four: Blend in with the crowd by wearing boring-looking clothes.

Superstar Spy!

ALLAN PINKERTON pioneered surveillance techniques in the nineteenth century that are still used today!

HIGH-TECHniques

New top secret technologies will help spies sleuth!

Biometrics

Collecting fingerprints is one of the oldest spy tricks in the book, but there are other types of biometric data spies use to identify a target, such as DNA (the unique biological code that makes each of us who we are) and eye scans (both irises and retinas can be scanned).

One hot biometric-tech trend is face recognition.

Information on faces is input into a supercomputer that in turn is connected to cameras. These cameras can now scan crowds for the faces of targets.

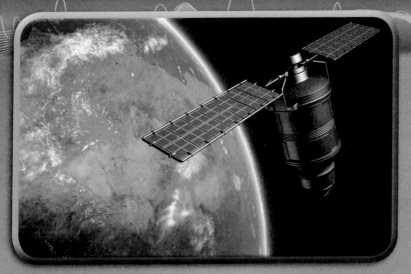

A communications satellite (also known as Comsat) orbits the earth.

Spy Satellites

Spy satellites have an eye on Earth—rain or shine. They can also spy on enemy spy satellites. Recent technology has made spy satellites nearly invisible to people on Earth. One day, face-recognition and spy-satellite technology could be combined so that faces could be clearly recognized from space.

100 Percent Face Recognition

Some sources speculate that the People's Republic of China is attempting to capture every citizen's face and place it in a face-recognition database that would be connected to its millions of surveillance cameras.

THE FUTURE IS NOW!
Cyber Espionage

Today's spies must be tech-savvy—modern spies spend more time sleuthing on the computer than anywhere else.

SPY LINGO
CYBER ESPIONAGE: Spying on computer systems to gather secrets.

Historic spies had to search desperately for clues and secrets. Now, clues and secrets are hidden in the massive piles of information that spies dig up from computers around the world.

Know The New Cyber Lingo!
So, how does cyber spying work?

> **HACKING** Breaking into a user's computer to see their files, and sometimes to control their computer.

< MALWARE Short for *malicious software*—a computer program that allows a spy to hack into a computer.

VIRUS DETECTED

>RAT Short for *remote access Trojan*—a type of malware that allows a spy to control your computer.

<SPEAR PHISHING

Spies get users to download malware onto their computer by creating fake e-mails that the target opens.

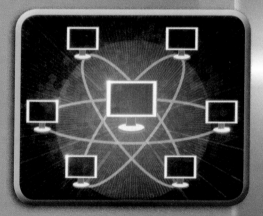

>BOTNETS Spies can control computers to send out more e-mails that contain more RATs to more computers!

This E-Mail Will Self-Destruct...

Some e-mail programs use a complex code to keep their e-mails safe, but if you really want to be secretive, set an e-mail to self-destruct at a certain time after it's sent.

GATHERING SECRETS FROM THE INTERNET

Spies may not even have to hack into a target's computer to learn more about them.
All they have to do is look online.

People are giving out secret information without even knowing it through Twitter, on their Facebook pages, in blogs, and other personal webpages.

For instance, military service members in Iraq uploaded pictures of themselves that were "geotagged" with their base's exact location. Enemy forces were able to execute an attack based on that information.

So, spies have to be very, VERY careful about what they say online—they never know who might be looking!

Having a secret identity—or a "cover"—is very important for spies to do their secret work.

ACTIVITY #1:
Internet Surveillance

The lead mad scientist from the country of Legendia, Dr. Crazypants, is planning on selling his secrets to evil forces! Intelligence reports say that he will meet with the evil forces on his next vacation, and it is your task to determine when and where that is.

SEARCH THROUGH DR. CRAZYPANTS'S BLOG POSTS, TWEETS, AND FACEBOOK PAGE TO FILL IN THE FOLLOWING INFORMATION:

Dr. Crazypants is going to meet with evil forces on
_____ at_____in_____!

(Check your answer at the bottom of page 17.)

Entry from crazy-legendia-scientist.tumblr.com
Dated 7/20/2013
I absolutely love Paris! What a wonderful place to get away and unwind. Here's a picture from my favorite spot in Paris— my favorite spot in the world, really. So beautiful at night, and an amazing meeting place—everyone knows how to get to it because they can see it from everywhere in the city!

Tweet on 8/29/2013
Dr. Crazypants @alldaycrazymd
FINALLY booked my #vacation. It's about time!
My favorite spot in the world!

Tweet on 9/5/2013
Dr. Crazypants @alldaycrazymd
Don't plan any surprise #birthday parties for me
this year. I'll be on #vacation! Plus, I hate surprises.

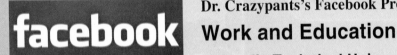

Dr. Crazypants's Facebook Profile

Work and Education

Legendia Technical University
Graduated magna cum laude with a PhD in Particle Physics

Xernon Corporation
Lead Scientist · Nation of Legendia · Feb 1989 to Present
I oversee a team of researchers in the area of experimental
science.

About Me
I love traveling through Europe, walking my dogs in the nearby
gorge, playing Mario Bros. on my original Nintendo (just LOVE that
Luigi!), and watching *The View*.

Basic Info

Birthday	October 1, 1968
Sex	Male
Relationship Status	Married to Victoria Crazypants
Languages	**Legendish** and **English**

Dr. Crazypants is going to meet with evil forces on October 1 at the Eiffel Tower in Paris!

SECTION TWO

COVERT COMMUNICATION TECHNIQUES

PASSING ALONG SECRETS

Once spies have collected all your juicy spy secrets, they have to pass the information back to headquarters.

But how do they do it safely and securely? Getting information out of enemy territory without being noticed is known as "covert communications."

I AM READY TO MEET AT B ON 1 OCT.
I CANNOT READ NORTH 13-19 SEPT.
IF YOU WILL MEET AT B ON 1 OCT. PLS SIGNAL NORTH 4 OF 20 SEPT TO CONFI. NO MESSAGE AT PIPE.
IF YOU CANNOT MEE. 1 OCT, SIGNAL NORTH AFTER 27 SEPT WITH MESSAGE AT PIPE.

Brush Pass

You need to pass along information to a fellow spy, but it's just too risky to meet. What can you do? Pick a very busy public place and quickly walk past each other, exchanging the information so fast that nobody notices.

Dead Drops

A dead drop is a secret location where a spy can hide information. A fellow spy comes by later to pick it up. Bricks, pipes, hollow logs, a hole in the wall— anything can be a dead drop. Spies have even used dead rats as a way to exchange information. Ewww!

One-Way Voice Link

HQ can send assignments to their agents in the field using shortwave radio. Because the agent doesn't radio back, their location will remain a mystery.

>>>>> CONCEALING

Cryptography
Speaking in Codes!

what is it?

Sending your message in code so your enemy can't understand it.

how is it done?

A key is created that determines how a message is encoded. Only someone who knows the key can decode the message.

blast from the past

In 400 B.C.E., Greeks hid messages underneath the wax of wax tablets.

During WWII, the Germans used this Enigma machine to encode messages.

The CIA's Invisible Ink

The CIA—America's international spy agency—just declassified its recipe for invisible ink, which it has been using since WWI!

SECRET MESSAGES

Steganography
Reading Between the Lines!

Hiding your message in another message that doesn't look like important information.

The message is hidden in another message that looks completely normal—a letter to your mother or a picture of your pet.

♥ A secret message is hidden within this photo.

E J 8 I L S K 9 S N
R L L 4 5 L J E N
A P O L W I 4 M
C J 3 U 9 D H E L N
Q O 4 9 N X S K J E N
O 5 6 N 3 R L
2 2 P L 3 9 F

∧ E-mail messages are encoded into a garble of letters, numbers, and characters.

Superstar Spy!

Mathematician Clifford Cocks of the British intelligence agency GCHQ is a pioneer of "public-key cryptography" which keeps many of today's digital technologies secure.

SECTION THREE

COVERS, DISGUISES, AND DOUBLE AGENTS

LIVING A DOUBLE LIFE...

Having a secret identity—or a "cover"—is very important for spies to do their secret work.

Forged Documents

Fake passports are a must for spies undercover, but other documents help add to a spy's legend: fake papers to apply for visas, fake diplomas, and even fake birth and marriage certificates.

SPY LINGO

ALIAS: The name you use undercover.

Keep Your Story Straight

Where were you born? Where did you go to school? Are you married? Do you have any hobbies? Talking about yourself undercover must sound natural and normal—and you have to back up your facts. If you say you like to scuba dive, you better not be afraid of water!

Blending In

The Russian KGB spy agency told its undercover officers not to wear sunglasses or trench coats—because that's what Hollywood spies look like!

SPY LINGO

LEGEND: The story you use about your cover—along with forged documents that back up your story.

Superstar Spy!

Sidney Rilley, the "Ace of Spies", worked for the British in the early 1900s. This real-life inspiration for James Bond went undercover on dangerous assignments around the globe, but always stayed cool.

MASTERS OF DISGUISE

Going Deeper Undercover

Sometimes you'll need a disguise so good that
not even your friends will know it's you!
The CIA has an entire department devoted to
disguise. Here are some of the things
that department has done.

Makeup, Masks and More

In the CIA's disguise
laboratory, makeup
and masks come
together to create
amazing disguises
for agents around the
globe. Every detail can be changed, from giving someone
a new nose to creating an entirely new face.

Code-Name Dagger

For spies on the go! A classified makeup kit, code-named "Dagger,"
can change a person's identity in a superfast five minutes.

Case Study: Argo

In order to rescue Americans from Iran in 1980, the CIA created one of the craziest and most detailed cover stories of all time—the fake Hollywood production of a sci-fi movie! The hostages then disguised themselves as the crew, and left the country safely!

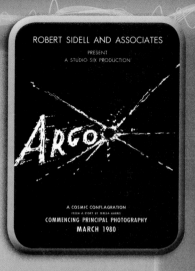

ROBERT SIDELL AND ASSOCIATES
PRESENT
A STUDIO SIX PRODUCTION

ARGO

A COSMIC CONFLAGRATION
FROM A STORY BY TERESA HARRIS
COMMENCING PRINCIPAL PHOTOGRAPHY
MARCH 1980

Superstar Spies!

ANTONIO & JONNA MENDEZ Husband and wife masters of disguise. He was in charge of the Argo mission, and she created the Dagger makeup kit. Check out Jonna's awesome disguise!

Before

After

Jonna Mendez works to transform this woman—into a man!

SOME PEOPLE JUST CAN'T

In the world of spying, it's important to build relationships with people "in the know." They help you get information on your targets and can give you a heads-up on dangerous situations.

Russian Spy Girl Anna Chapman

This spy was discovered in New York City in 2010 and deported. She was a regular in the NYC club scene and is now a model and TV personality in Russia.

(In)Famous American Informant

JOHN ANTHONY WALKER was a naval officer and the KGB's number one informant—and the most damaging spy in modern US history.

KEEP A SECRET....

SPY LINGO
DOUBLE AGENT: An informant that works for your enemy's spy agency.

During the Cold War, the US and USSR both had a number of double agents getting the inside scoop.

Russian Double Agent

OLEG PENKOVSKY, KGB officer, provided Americans with information so important, he may have prevented war!

American Double Agents

ALDRICH AMES gave the KGB information including the names of the CIA's Russian informants.

FBI agent ROBERT HANSSEN gave the KGB the most information of any American double agent.

I-Spy Foreign-Language Skills

Learning foreign languages lets you speak with informants around the globe. Pick up another language (or seven) now and spiff up your spy skills!

CASE STUDY

OPERATION NEPTUNE SPEAR

Catching bin Laden

The CIA used many of the techniques mentioned in this book to catch the terrorist behind the 9/11 attacks.

Foreign-Language Skills

Agents found their way to bin Laden because they were able to speak multiple languages and blend into local cultures.

Stakeouts/Tailing

Bin Laden's personal courier was followed by the CIA. He led them to the town of Abbottabad and the bin Laden compound there.

Superstar Spy!

Nobody knows her real name—it's still classified—but the fearless CIA agent with the alias of "Maya" led the search for bin Laden.

Hacking Al-Qaeda

The bin Laden compound didn't have Internet or telephone! But many websites have been set up and used by the terrorist organization bin Laden led: Al-Qaeda. British intelligence hacked one magazine's website and replaced the recipe for a bomb with a recipe for a cupcake.

Spy Satellites

Spy satellites confirmed that bin Laden had built a compound in Abbottabad, Pakistan.

Audio Surveillance

The CIA may have even used a "laser listener," a device that can listen in on conversations from far away by using a laser to sense audio vibrations on a window.

Biometrics

Facial recognition and DNA were used to identify bin Laden.

HOW SPY-SAVVY ARE YOU?

ACTIVITY #2:
Spy Quiz!

Below are five different problems you could face as a spy. Choose from three solutions to test your spy skills.

On the bottom of the next page, upside down, point values are assigned to each answer. (No peeking!) Add up your spy points and find out how spy-savvy you really are.

1) There's going to be a police exercise in the park at the same time you had planned a brush pass. You . . .
    a) Keep the meeting.
    b) Send a coded message to your contact to meet when the exercise is over.
    c) Slip the information into an envelope for overnight delivery.

2) You're tailing a target that turns around and looks you right in the face. You . . .
    a) Calmly turn to look at a store window.
    b) Ask him how his day is going.
    c) Scream.

3) You need to gain access to a target's computer. You . . .
   a) Try to slip into his office while he's in the bathroom.
   b) Call his secretary and let him know that a spy agency would like to speak with him.
   c) Hack his boss's e-mail account and send him a message with a RAT.

4) You have only five minutes to change your identity before escaping from enemy territory. You . . .
   a) Open your top secret Dagger makeup kit.
   b) Shave your head, and then use the hair to make a mustache.
   c) Throw on a hat.

5) You have just intercepted a letter from your target to his mother. You . . .
   a) Suddenly miss your mother.
   b) Burn it.
   c) Check for a message written in invisible ink.

If you scored . . .

5–8 POINTS—You should probably not become a spy . . . but keep studying.

9–11 POINTS—With a little work, you might become a top operative.

12–15 POINTS—YES! Call the CIA now! You should be a spy.

Learn More Top Secret Techniques at these Spy Museums!

INTERNATIONAL SPY MUSEUM
Washington, Dc
The largest number of spy artifacts ever assembled for public viewing. Features a Spy Camp for aspiring KidSpy recruits.

SPY AND PRIVATE-EYE MUSEUM
Austin, Tx
Cold War-era 1960s and 1970s gadgets, and even older artifacts like antique reports from Allan Pinkerton's agency.

P.I. MUSEUM
San Diego, Ca
Historical private-investigator artifacts from the 1890s, 1940s, and present day. Catch the P.I. Museum on Wheels as it travels around the country.